LAND OF GIANTS

LAND OF GIANTS
WILL BURRARD-LUCAS

TSAVO TRUST

For Primrose and Benjamin

CONTENTS

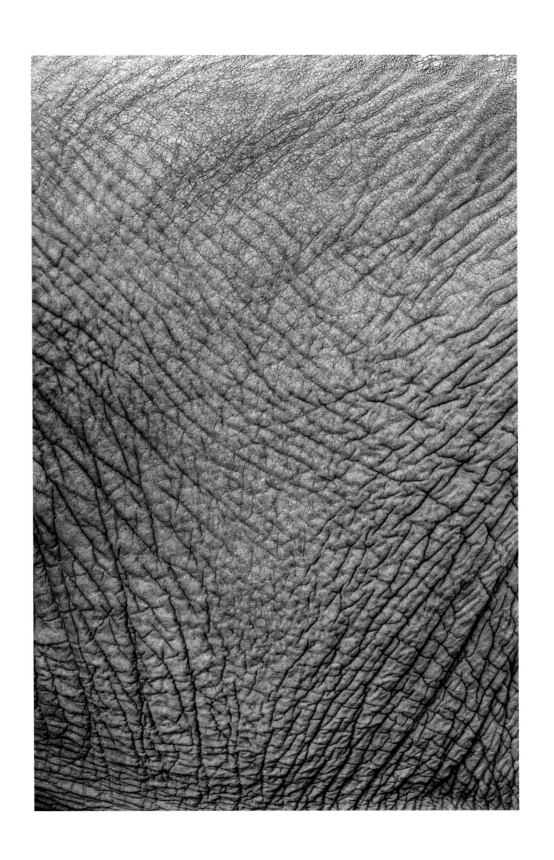

FOREWORD

Ian Craig, MBS, OBE
Director of Conservation, Northern Rangelands Trust

Browsing through Land of Giants, I am brought instantly into a world that lives alongside us every day, yet is now entirely dependant on our goodwill.

The images so skilfully captured through Will Burrard-Lucas' lens portray a complex society that has evolved to live with the seasons, moving across the vast, often harsh, yet beautiful landscape of Tsavo, based on decisions rooted in generations. Amongst this society are icons – icons that once were common across the continent, individual goliaths amongst giants, bulls and cows that evolved over generations through genetics and good nutrition to carry ivory larger than all their compatriots. The sight of great sweeping tusks carried by these elegant architects of nature command a respect captured in the reverence that these are the real elders of nature – they have achieved the privilege of growing old in a world so greedy for ivory.

Land of Giants captures a moment in time where senior world leaders led by China have come together to ban the sale of ivory – this has been reflected in a short few years in ivory values dropping and a reduction in poaching. Perhaps these giants can now look forward to a future unmolested by AK-47s, free to spread their genes and roam the vast expanses of Tsavo.

I applaud Richard Moller and Will Burrard-Lucas for lifting the veil on the mystery and myth of the Giants of Tsavo. Where once only stories were told of the Tuskers of Tsavo – now they are known and respected individuals, valued and safe thanks to the dedication of the Tsavo Trust team and their partnership with Kenya Wildlife Service.

Thank you for sharing these extraordinary images with those of us unable to witness their majestic presence.

TSAVO TRUST

Richard Moller
Co-founder and CEO, Tsavo Trust

The Tsavo Conservation Area comprises 20,000 square kilometres of dispersal area and 22,000 square kilometres of National Park, representing 49% of Kenya's total protected land. This vast, mostly roadless expanse of wilderness provides precious habitat for an array of species and great potential for wildlife growth. It is a rare natural resource in a world where wild areas are shrinking at an alarming rate.

Tsavo is home to the largest population of elephants in Kenya – estimated at almost thirteen thousand individuals as of the 2017 aerial census. However, Tsavo's elephants are facing a number of threats. With a rapidly expanding human population, most dispersal areas are becoming increasingly utilised by humans with little tolerance towards elephants. Tsavo has also suffered significant elephant poaching over the years. A population estimated to be over 45,000 elephants in the early 1970's plummeted to fewer than 6,000 by 1989.

The formation of Kenya Wildlife Service (KWS), and the imposition of the international ivory trade ban in 1989, reversed the trend and twenty years of stability saw the elephant population bounce back. Sadly, poaching has returned with a vengeance in the last decade and this has placed the elephants, particularly those with big tusks, at huge risk. Without urgent and concerted conservation action, Tsavo's elephants and an irreplaceable piece of Kenya's National Heritage could be lost forever.

Opposite: Richard Moller patrolling a remote corner of Tsavo in a Super Cub aeroplane.

Founded in December 2012, Tsavo Trust is a Kenyan, field-based, not-for-profit conservation organisation. Its aim is to provide meaningful support to Kenya Wildlife Service in conserving and managing wildlife resources, combatting wildlife crime and supporting specific key communities that border the Parks within the Tsavo Conservation Area.

A key component of Tsavo Trust's support of KWS is the provision of aerial and ground assistance. This relates not only to monitoring and data collection, but also helping to mount rapid responses to imminent poaching threats.

A second strand is Tsavo Trust's continued development and stewardship of self-governing, community-led wildlife conservancies in key areas within the Tsavo Conservation Area. The aim of this is ultimately to create secure buffers bordering the National Park at the same time as generating economic opportunities for marginalized communities.

The establishment of an effective field base has facilitated Tsavo Trust's operations as well as provided an invaluable platform for Tsavo Trust's partners. The fostering of close partnerships with other like-minded organisations working in support of wildlife, habitats and communities has always been a fundamental component of Tsavo Trust's agenda.

Opposite: A Tsavo Trust vehicle and Kenya Wildlife Service helicopter converge on a bull elephant during an operation to place satellite tracking collars on twenty elephants living in areas of human-wildlife conflict, February 2018.

IN SEARCH OF TSAVO'S GIANTS

Will Burrard-Lucas

The Tsavo Trust Land Rover rattled over the corrugated dirt road leading into Tsavo East National Park. I have that familiar feeling in the pit of my stomach; excitement that I might soon come face to face with a creature I have journeyed so far to see, anxiety that today might be another day that would come and go without result. After all, we are looking for a needle in a haystack; a single animal in an area the size of Switzerland.

Kyalo's mobile phone starts to ring. He brings the car to a halt and takes the call. On the other end is Richard Moller, CEO of Tsavo Trust.

Kyalo speaks briefly in Swahili and hangs up. "Richard's found her," he says with a grin. I feel a surge of exhilaration but I try not to get my hopes up; years of searching for elusive wildlife have taught me not to count my chickens before they hatch.

We turn off the main road down a narrow track flanked with dust-clad vegetation; an impenetrable tangle of twigs and branches, long-since stripped of leaves by an army of browsing impala, gerenuks, kudu and giraffes.

After 30 minutes, we catch sight of Richard's Super Cub aeroplane circling ahead. Richard's voice comes through on the radio. "I'm above her now," he says.

Kyalo swings the Land Rover off the sandy track towards the circling aircraft and starts weaving left and right, seeking an unobstructed path through the dense vegetation. My eyes strain to catch a glimpse of an elephant but the bush is too thick.

F_MU1 photographed for the first time with BeetleCam, August 2017.

We emerge out into a dusty clearing and Richard's voice comes through again, "She's heading your way, you should be able to see her".

Over the bushes I catch a glimpse of an elephant's back. Seconds later she steps out into the open and I am left speechless.

In front of me is an elephant known to Tsavo Trust as F_MU1. She is skinny and old but strides forward with stately grace. It is her ivory though that makes her truly exceptional. Each tusk reaches all the way down to the ground. She is like a relic from a bygone era and unlike any elephant I've ever seen before. In some ways she is more impressive than a big male tusker because her ivory is so long in comparison to her body size.

As a wildlife photographer, finding a subject like this is incredibly rare; a creature that is unique – probably the most remarkable of her kind – and yet an animal that few people even know exists.

We stay with her for the rest of the morning and she leads us to an isolated waterhole. It is the height of a gruelling dry season and many elephants are gathered here, delighting in the cool water. Many will have wandered so far in search of food that it may have been two or three days since they last drank.

F_MU1 patiently awaits her turn at the water. The terrain is flat and open, a perfect opportunity for me to deploy BeetleCam, my remote-control camera buggy. With this, I want to get close-up wide-angle images showing her amazing tusks stretching down towards the camera.

I gradually edge the buggy into position in front of her and she contemplates it benignly. I look down at the live image on my wireless monitor and have to pinch myself – I can scarcely believe that this photograph I have envisaged for so long is about to materialise! It is a feeling of privilege and euphoria that I will never forget.

Searching for LU1 from the Tsavo Trust Super Cub, August 2017.

Two weeks later and we are on the search for another of Tsavo's iconic elephants, this time a bull known by the codename LU1. If F_MU1 was the queen of Tsavo, LU1 would be the undisputed king. He is at least 50 years old and it's estimated his tusks weigh well over 100lbs each – perhaps more than 130lbs – making him the largest tusker in Tsavo, and possibly the world.

This time I have joined Richard in the Super Cub and we are quartering the land, peering down into the bush, hoping to catch sight of an elephant with magnificent ivory gleaming in the early morning light.

We have been flying every morning for a week and have spotted LU1 a couple of times, but I haven't yet been able to photograph him on the ground. On the last occasion we spotted him from the air and immediately landed at the nearest airstrip where Kyalo met us in the Land Rover. We spent the rest of the day scraping the vehicle through the thick bush as we attempted to get close to him. However, he hasn't reached this ripe old age without being extremely canny and it was impossible for us to get close enough for a clear shot.

A weathered inselberg looms in front of us and we climb slightly so that the top of the rocky outcrop is level with our wingtip. Richard points out a jumble of old stone walls and his voice crackles over the intercom. "Those are from the First World War," he explains, "fortifications to defend the railway from the Germans in Tanzania."

Most days we have flown over the railway, which bisects the Tsavo Conservation Area and separates Tsavo East from Tsavo West National Park. This strategic line, built between 1896 and 1901, links the port of Mombasa with Nairobi. While construction was taking place near the Tsavo River, a pair of maneless male lions gained notoriety as the "Man-eaters of Tsavo" after they stalked and killed at least 28 construction workers.

We finally spot LU1 in an area we had flown over more than two hours earlier – he must have been under a tree when we passed overhead the first time. We note the direction he is travelling and head to the landing strip.

Attempting to get near the old tusker again in the Land Rover would be futile, so today we are going to leave the safety of the vehicle behind and try our luck on foot.

Coming face-to-face with LU1 for the first time, August 2017.

We drive to a spot about a kilometre from where we spotted LU1 and set off into the bush. Richard leads the way while I follow a few paces behind.

We cautiously approach a thicket in front of where we estimate the elephant was heading. We are very vigilant because we don't quite know where he is now.

Richard climbs a tree and glimpses LU1's back sticking up above the bushes 250m away. He is with a younger bull and they are moving towards us. We will have to keep tabs on the second bull because he could be every bit as dangerous as the tusker. We are outside the National Park and the elephants know that this is not a safe area for them. This makes them especially edgy.

Richard descends and kicks the ground gently to raise a small puff of dust. We watch as a slight breeze carries the dust away from the elephants. It is imperative that we stay down wind of elephants; if either one catches our scent then our chance of getting close will be blown.

We set off on a tangent, aiming to intersect the path that LU1 seemed to be taking. As we move we check the ground before every step so as to avoid snapping a twig or crunching a dried leaf.

We flush a diminutive dik-dik and it nimbly darts away. Fortunately, the tiny antelope doesn't let out its high-pitched alarm call and so the elephants aren't alerted to our presence.

As we get closer, we start to use the bushes for cover. Elephants don't have great eyesight but at this range they would easily spot a human out in the open. Before making any move, Richard plans an escape route; if one of the elephants were to charge us now, we would need to be able to quickly dash for cover behind a suitable obstacle.

It is late morning and the temperature is rising. There is a shady acacia tree behind us and Richard thinks that the elephants will shelter under it during the hottest part of the day. We position ourselves between the elephants and the tree and wait.

Just as predicted, LU1 comes towards us and at last emerges into the open. It is only up close that the true bulk of this magnificent animal becomes apparent. I start taking photographs and am thankful that my new mirrorless camera has a completely silent electronic shutter.

My last encounter with F_MU1 showing the Tsavo Trust Land Rover in the background, August 2017.

LU1 strolls forwards and still hasn't noticed the two humans crouching beside the bush. Richard whispers that we have to back up as he's getting too close. I edge backwards and the elephant instantly senses the movement. He curls up his trunk and for a brief instant takes a hesitant backwards step – he still hasn't caught our scent and is unsure what we are. Then he rushes towards us in a mock charge, dust billowing up from under his feet. It is frightening how fast he covers the ground. He pulls up a couple of metres short of where I had been crouching, but by now we have already fallen back and there is a large termite mound between him and us.

The old elephant turns away and melts back into the undergrowth. Now that his guard is up, we won't get close to him again today so we retrace our steps back to the vehicle. It was an exhilarating encounter and I am elated to have been able to capture clear images of another of Tsavo's giants.

Over the weeks that followed, I would head deeper into this land of giants and come face to face with a handful of other remarkable elephants. I would also have further opportunities to photograph LU1.

As for F_MU1, I photographed her several more times during the month of August 2017 and she proved to be the most exceptional subject. Her temperament was always gentle and calm. Sometimes she would come within touching distance of our Land Rover.

A couple of months later I received word from Richard that F_MU1's carcass had been found. She had succumbed to the drought and died of starvation. It was desperately sad news, but a small triumph at least that she had reached a ripe old age and that her life hadn't been ended prematurely by a poacher's bullet, poison arrow or snare.

Tsavo's elephants are under great pressure from conflict with man and of course poaching. However, Tsavo Trust, in partnership with Kenya Wildlife Service, are performing incredible work and I have high hopes that elephants like F_MU1 and LU1 will continue to exist in Tsavo's vast wilderness for a long time to come.

ELEPHANTS OF TSAVO

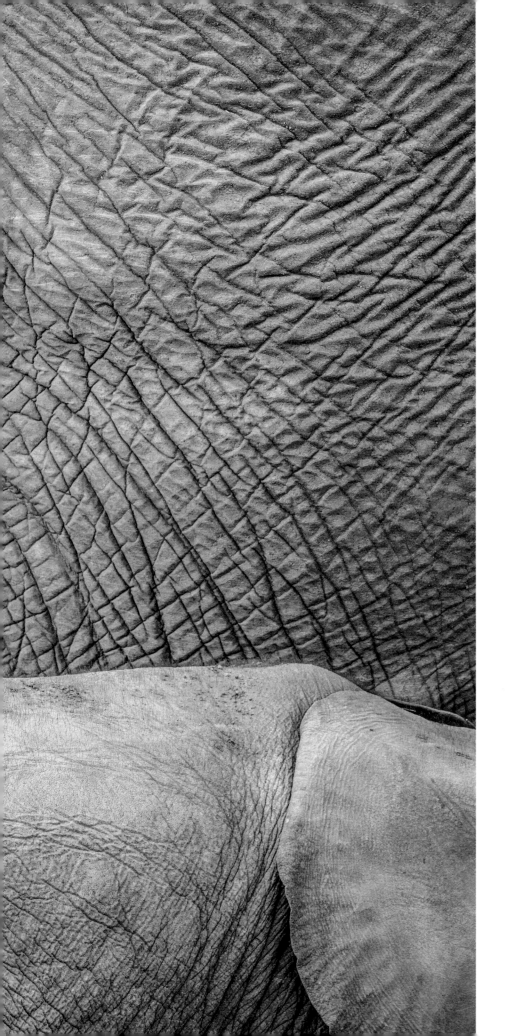

Folio II
MATRIARCHS

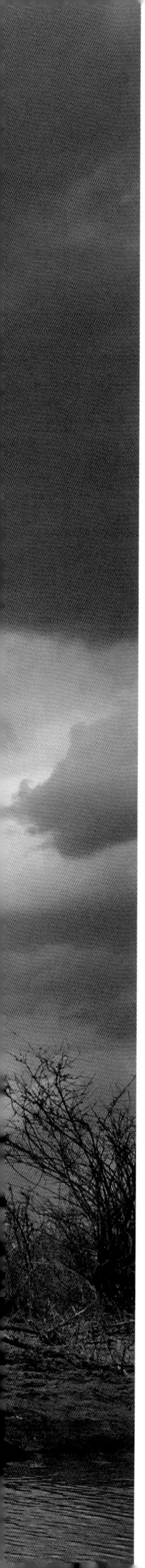

Folio III

BULLS

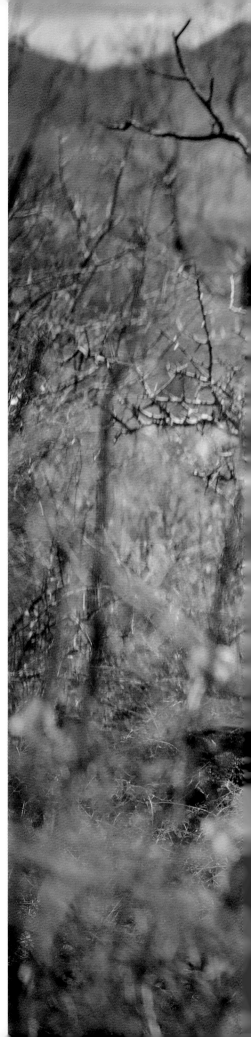

BeetleCam in action next to a waterhole, August 2017.

PHOTOGRAPHER'S NOTE

Will Burrard-Lucas

When I embarked on this project, I knew it was not going to be easy to capture enough images of sufficient quality and variety to justify an entire book solely focusing on elephants. I was also acutely aware that elephants have been photographed in such depth, and by so many incredible photographers, that finding a fresh angle required to make this book stand out was going to be an even tougher challenge.

Fortunately, my task was made immeasurably easier by Richard Moller and Tsavo Trust, since with their help I was able to find and photograph some of the most remarkable elephants left on Earth. This included unique cow tuskers such as F_MU1 and F_DI1 and the big bull tuskers such as LU1 and WS1. With each tusk weighing more than 100lbs (45kg), there are now less than twenty of these big bull tuskers left in the whole of Africa.

In the hope of capturing intimate images, I came equipped with some of my own innovations, including BeetleCam, my remote-control camera buggy. While the close-up, wide-angle look has now become fairly commonplace in wildlife photography, I felt that there was still scope to push the boundaries further in search of fresh perspectives. In particular, replacing the DSLR camera on BeetleCam with a mirrorless camera allowed me to transmit the image from the camera's sensor back to a small wireless monitor in real-time. It was almost as if I had my eye to the camera's electronic viewfinder and I was able to compose photographs with greater accuracy and produce images with precise framing such as those shown on pages 40, 42, 67 and 91.

BeetleCam allowed me to capture wide-angle photographs in the range of 16 to 24mm. To obtain other perspectives, I employed different techniques and equipment: aerial images taken with a 24-70mm or 70-200mm from the Super Cub light aircraft; 400mm telephoto images taken from the Land Rover; and medium-range images taken with a 70-200mm whilst sneaking up close on foot.

The black and white images in this book are a departure from my normal colour photography and represent the advent of a new chapter in my journey as a photographer. Black and white brings drama back to dusty landscapes and the hazy skies of the African dry season. It also reveals forms and textures wonderfully and is thus an ideal medium for a series focusing on wrinkly old elephants!

In processing the images for this book, I have adhered to a predominantly documentary ethos. Therefore, the images have been converted to black and white but are otherwise faithful to the scenes as they appeared through my viewfinder. The exception to this is the composite image on the page opposite, which I created to simply illustrate the size of the elephant. In a handful of images I have removed small distractions such as a branch or blade of grass. A few images are panoramas, created by stitching together two or more images taken at the same time, in order to give a wider field of view than my lens would otherwise allow.

I could have kept working on this project forever! I never grew tired of spending time in the company of elephants – in fact the opposite was true; the more time I spent with these complex giants, the more I started to feel a deep affinity towards them. They really are the most wonderful, intelligent and magnificent of animals.

Ultimately, I hope this book succeeds in its intended purpose of highlighting the treasures of Tsavo and supporting Tsavo Trust and Kenya Wildlife Service in their efforts to protect this Land of Giants.

Opposite: I photographed LU1 sheltering under an acacia tree and waited for him to move off before taking an identical image of myself under the tree. I then created this composite image to illustrate the size of this magnificent elephant.

BIG TUSKER PROJECT

Richard Moller
Co-founder and CEO, Tsavo Trust

Historically, elephants carrying tusks weighing in excess of 100lbs (45kg) per side were known as "hundred pounders" and were much sought after by hunters and poachers alike. They were also a draw for many visiting tourists to Kenya. The famous elephant of Marsabit National Park known as "Ahmed" in the 1970's is a classic example of an iconic tusker who became so famous that he went on to enjoy a permanent Presidential Security Decree with round the clock protection. He lived out his full life and died of old age – a rare occurrence in today's elephant world.

In 2018, at least nine super tuskers can be found in Tsavo alongside 23 emerging bull tuskers who will be the "hundred pounders" of the future. There are also four iconic cow tuskers with ivory reaching down to the ground. It is the protection from ivory poachers of these last iconic animals which provides the rationale behind the Tsavo Trust's Big Tusker Project.

Between 2014 and 2017, Tsavo lost a third of its big tuskers to either old age, drought, Human Elephant Conflict or poaching. Despite this trend, more "big tuskers" can be found in Tsavo than anywhere else in Africa and arguably the area holds the last sustainable gene pool of large tuskers on Earth. If the future of these elephants is not secured today, they could soon be gone forever.

Opposite: While the elephant WS1 is sedated, a team from Tsavo Trust, Save the Elephants and Kenya Wildlife Service record data, fit a satellite tracking collar and treat an old wound inflicted by a poacher's arrow. Of the twenty elephants collared in this operation, nine had old spear or arrow wounds.

The overarching goal of the Tsavo Trust's Big Tusker Project is to save the remaining iconic large bull and cow elephants of Tsavo by providing enhanced elephant security and monitoring within the Tsavo Conservation Area in support of Kenya Wildlife Service, providing "eyes in the sky" and "eyes and ears on the ground" through the following operations:

    (a) regular aerial monitoring and ground team backup through reconnaissance flights;

    (b) biodiversity protection and de-snaring through mobile ground teams;

    (c) research and monitoring through mobile ground teams;

    (d) enhancing intelligence and investigations capabilities;

    (e) long-term engagement with specific communities that border the National Parks;

    (f) enhancing and developing further conservation partnerships where KWS take the lead role.

Special emphasis is placed on locating and monitoring Tsavo's big tuskers and maintaining a regular aerial and ground presence in order to deter poachers planning to target these iconic animals and the emerging tuskers.

The Big Tusker Project aerial and ground operations do come at a significant cost, and in order for them to be maintained, Tsavo Trust relies on donor funding. Tsavo Trust hope to at least maintain their current Big Tusker Project operations, as long as the threat to these elephants remains. Much, much more can be done with further funding, such as increased number of hours in the air, further mobile ground support teams, various infrastructural support projects to complement KWS, engagement with local communities, training and capacity building within Tsavo Trust and its partners. To help Tsavo Trust and KWS to conserve the Big Tuskers of Tsavo, please consider donating to the cause. More information can be found at tsavotrust.org.

The preceding pages of this book contain unique photographs showing four of Tsavo's bull tuskers (including LU1, the largest of all) and two cow tuskers. On pages 207 to 209 is an index, which identifies all the photographs containing one of these spectacular animals.

Opposite: The tusker WS1 standing up after being fitted with a new satellite tracking collar. The data from this collar will inform anti-poaching efforts and provide insights into the growing issue of human-elephant conflict in the region.

MEET THE TUSKERS

F_DI1 *(Cow)*

Pages: 52, 126 – 139

F_MU1 *(Cow)*

Pages: 16, 92 – 123

LU1 *(Bull)*

Pages: 6, 20, 22, 142, 153 – 162, 165 – 168, 171 – 176, 178, 179, 194, 200, 222

WS1 *(Bull)*

Pages: 151, 164, 191, 197, 202, 204

KO1 *(Bull)*

Page: 183

IL1 *(Bull)*

Page: 187

INDEX OF PHOTOGRAPHS

2017

Page 22

2017

Page 26

2017

Page 29

2017

Page 30

2018

Page 31

2018

Page 32

2018

Page 33

2017

Page 34

2017

Page 35

2017

Page 37

2017

Page 38

2017

Page 40

2017

Page 42

2017

Page 43

2017

Page 45

2017

Page 46

2017

Page 47

2017

Page 48

2017

Page 49

2017

Page 51

2018

Page 52

2018

Page 53

2017

Page 55

2017

Page 56

2017

Page 57

2017

Page 58

2017

Page 59

2017

Page 60

2017

Page 61

2017

Page 63

2017

Page 64

2017

Page 65

2017

Page 66

2017

Page 67

2017

Page 68

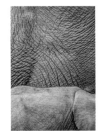

2017

Page 69

2017

Page 69

2018

Page 70

2018

Page 72

2018

Page 74

2018

Page 75

2017

Page 76

2017

Page 77

2017

Page 79

2017

Page 80

2017

Page 81

2017

Page 85

2017

Page 86

2017

Page 87

2017

Page 88

2017

Page 91

2017

Page 92

2017

Page 94

2017

Page 95

2017

Page 97

2017

Page 98

2017

Page 99

2017

Page 100

2017

Page 101

2017

Page 102

2017

Page 103

2017

Page 104

2017

Page 105

2017

Page 106

2017

Page 108

2017

Page 109

2017

Page 111

2017

Page 112

2017

Page 113

2017

Page 114

2017

Page 115

2017

Page 116

2017

Page 117

2017

Page 118

2017

Page 121

2017

Page 122

2017

Page 123

2017

Page 125

2018

Page 127

2018

Page 128

2018

Page 129

2018

Page 131

2018

Page 132

2018

Page 133

2018

Page 135

2018

Page 136

2018

Page 137

2018

Page 139

2017

Page 142

2017

Page 144

2017

Page 146

2017

Page 147

2017

Page 148

2018

Page 151

2018

Page 152

2018

Page 153

2018

Page 154

2018

Page 156

2018

Page 157

2018

Page 159

2018

Page 160

2018

Page 161

2017

Page 162

2018

Page 164

2018

Page 165

2018

Page 166

2018

Page 167

2018

Page 168

2018

Page 170

2018

Page 171

2018

Page 172

2018

Page 174

2018

Page 175

2018

Page 176

2018

Page 177

2018

Page 178

2018

Page 179

2018

Page 180

2018

Page 181

2017

Page 182

2017

Page 183

2017

Page 184

2017

Page 185

2017

Page 187

2018

Page 188

2018

Page 190

2018

Page 191

2018

Page 192

2018

Page 194

2018

Page 195

2018

Page 197

2017

Page 198

2017

Page 200

2018

Page 202

2018

Page 204

2018

Page 207

2017

Page 207

2018

Page 208

2018

Page 208

2017

Page 209

2017

Page 209

2018

Page 222

2018

Page 224

ACKNOWLEDGEMENTS

I would like to thank the following people and organisations for their invaluable assistance:

Chris Gordon for first introducing me to Richard and for your support both during this project and subsequently.

Richard Moller for your tireless work protecting Tsavo's treasures and for being the driving force behind this project.

Vanessa Moller, Alia, Tiva, Tamara, James, Mindi and **Russell** for your kind hospitality in Mtito Andei.

The Tembo 2 team: **Kyalo, Katana** and **Christine**, for your hard work, patience and dedication in the field; you played a critical role in many of the images featured in this book!

Josh Outran for your excellent piloting and support from the air.

The other employees of **Tsavo Trust** for your assistance, hospitality and your efforts to protect Tsavo.

Kenya Wildlife Service for generously supporting this endeavour.

Ian Craig for kindly writing the foreword to this book.

Sony and **The World Photography Organisation** for the grant that funded my initial fieldwork.

Mike Kirkland and **Satao Camp** for hosting me for part of my time in Tsavo.

And finally my family: **Nat, Primrose, Benjamin, Mum, Dad, TC, Maureen, Megan** and **Matthew** for your unwavering support.

LAND OF GIANTS
By Will Burrard-Lucas

Photographs, text & design © 2017-2018 Will Burrard-Lucas
Foreword © 2018 Ian Craig
Tsavo Trust, Big Tusker Project text © 2018 Richard Moller

Produced by Burrard-Lucas Books
http://books.burrard-lucas.com/

in partnership with Tsavo Trust
http://www.tsavotrust.org/

and Kenya Wildlife Service
http://www.kws.go.ke/

Printed and bound in China.

ISBN: 978-1-912751-00-6

First Edition
10 9 8 7 6 5 4 3 2 1

www.landofgiantsbook.com